The Power In You

Releasing the supernatural power of God to work through you

by
Donald Shorter Sr.

Harrison House
Tulsa, Oklahoma

The Power In You
ISBN 0-89274-978-4
Copyright © 1996 by Donald Shorter Sr.
P.O. Box 44800
Tacoma, Washington 98444

Published by Harrison House, Inc.
P.O. Box 35035
Tulsa, Oklahoma 74153

Contents

Dedication

This book is dedicated to my father and mother in the faith, Drs. Frederick K. C. and Betty Price. Their examples of simple faith and patience have paid off in a big way in the life of my wife and I, our family, and ministry. We thank God for you two excellent, godly examples in the body of Christ.

Introduction

While in prayer one day, the Lord dropped four simple words into my heart. As soon as I heard them I immediately received a visual impression in my spirit of what God was saying to me. Then I sought for and received more understanding. But I had no idea that these four words could mean so much to so many people around the world. The words were, *"the power in you."* God's power in you can change the world.

> **Now unto him that is able to do exceeding abundantly above all that we ask or think, according to the power that worketh in us.**
>
> **Ephesians 3:20**

These words of the apostle Paul out of his letter to the Ephesians will help you understand how God's power can work within you to make you victorious in life. As you discover how to tap into His power and allow Him to work through you, you will be able to change most things around you. You will be able to overcome any hindrance or obstacle in life.

God's power is always ready to help you turn adverse situations into great victories. The power I am referring to is the gift of God's Holy Spirit, who dwells in every believer **who receives Him**. He will dwell in you, and will be with you as your Comforter.

The Spirit of God, is not an *it*, He is the person of the Holy Spirit who works through the lives of the believers in which He dwells. The truth in this book will help transform ordinary people into powerful men and women capable of changing circumstances in their communities and cities.

My first encounter with the reality of this powerful bit of Scripture in Ephesians 3:20 occurred one day when I received a phone call from one of our church members. She was one of our intercessors who worked as a nurse. I heard concern, desperation, and urgency in her voice. And I realized that what she was sharing had to be dealt with immediately as she described one of the most hopeless situations I had ever faced as a young pastor.

While making her rounds in the cancer ward in the hospital at which she worked, this born-again, Spirit-filled nurse struck up a conversation with one of her patients. The doctors had given this patient a very short time to live. Before being stricken with cancer, she was young, full of life, and had been very active. But now she had it settled in her mind that she had to die, because it was God's will to die — to give Him the glory. But this intercessor, who had been taught differently, was not going to accept the doctor's science as the final word.

So the nurse told this young woman that if she would receive God's Word and be prayed for, God could completely heal her. She then convinced this woman that she could be healed, and set up a phone appointment between the patient and me. I will never forget receiving that phone call! As soon as I began to talk with her, I could hear the spirit of unbelief speaking. She really did believe that it was God's will for her to die, even though she would leave her husband and several children. But as I ministered, the Holy Spirit brought Ephesians 3:20 to my mind:

> Now unto him that is able to do exceeding abundantly above all that we ask or think, *according to the power that worketh in us.*
>
> Ephesians 3:20

She later told me as I quoted that Scripture and spoke the word "**power**" to her that she felt something go through her, and that immediately something began to happen to her. From that time on, she kept hearing the word, "**power**" ring in her mind. Then, she began to make a desperate life-changing confession that was contrary to her previous religious teaching. And she began to say continually to herself, "I want this **power** to work in me."

As we concluded our phone call, I invited her to come to our next service on Wednesday night. I told her that after the service we would pray for God to complete the work He had begun in her so she could receive her complete healing. Both she and her husband came early the next Wednesday, and at the end of the service, my wife, myself, and one of our assistants met with them.

This woman was very swollen from her treatments, had lost most of her hair, and had many tubes in her body. When I began to teach her again on what the power of Ephesians 3:20 means, she told me she had been studying the verse since I had shared it over the phone. After ministering the Word to her, we laid hands on her and prayed. Then, we cursed the cancer and called forth the life of God into her body. When we were finished, she and her husband went home believing that they had received.

The woman had a regularly scheduled hospital appointment set for Friday, but that Friday as she headed to the hospital, something was different. This time, she had faith in the Word of God, and was speaking to herself a life-changing confession that God's power was now working within her.

During the appointment, the doctors ran the usual tests, but this time the woman noticed that they appeared to be perplexed at what they were finding. After this examination, the doctors informed the woman that they couldn't find one bit of cancer anywhere in her body! She was totally healed by the power of God!

This all took place several years ago, and since that time she has remained completely healed of cancer by God's power in her!

God is no respecter of persons, conditions, or names of diseases. No matter what situation you may be dealing with, the power of God will work in you, as It did in this woman. As you read this book, *His* power will change *your* hopeless situation!

Preface

The Holy Spirit

If you are born again, you have the opportunity to be baptized in the Holy Spirit and welcome inside of you a supernatural person who will change your personality. The reason your personality can be changed is because of what I call your person-ability. The person you are on the inside of you dictates the *ability* you have regarding the situations operating outside of you. If the strengths of the person operating on the inside of you are very small, weak, selfish, corrupt, unclean, or fearful, these characteristics will be reflected. But when the Holy Spirit is resident in you, you have a *great* reservoir of power.

The Holy Spirit is a person Who lives in you. When He lives in you, you are no longer stifled by relying on your own personal ability to assure your success. Now you can rely on the person of the Holy Spirit — the same person God Himself uses to carry out His vision. Now you have the ability to become a different kind of person because of the Holy Spirit in you, in spite of your own frailties and lack of personal ability. In fact, as you yield more and more to the person of the Holy Spirit, you will become more like Him. This means that your abilities will be enhanced by God's power. After all, this was God's original plan when He created His children.

I believe Christians who are truly living according to the direction of the Spirit of God shouldn't suffer from a poor self-image, because their image is now associated with the image of God:

> **And God said, Let us make man in our image, after
> our likeness: and let them** [all of them, male and female]
> **have dominion....**
>
> Genesis 1:26

It was God's original intention for man to live in complete dominion. This was possible because man came out of God. He was a part of God and was given dominion because of his God-ordained position. God made man in His own image, then placed his God-originated soul and spirit into a body made out of the earth. But Adam's disobedience made him fall into sin in the Garden of Eden, and he lost his original position that God had designed for him. His disobedience not only separated him from God, it separated Adam from his dominion. But the good news of the Gospel is that Jesus came to restore man back to the original position God had planned for him — a position of dominion!

A Spiritual Transaction

To be restored from the fall, man had to be restored to the One he came from — God. Therefore, a spiritual transaction takes place when you are born again. Your spirit is reconnected to God and you are again attached to Him as the *source* of your appointed dominion is restored. But how many born-again Christians truly understand that?

Imagine for a moment a set of musical drums that are being used as large cooking pots and pans for the kitchen. They may serve this purpose, but the original purpose for which they were created was to be used as drums. You can say drums are deep and round like cooking pots and pans, and they sit on a stove like pots and pans. But the only reason you could even imagine them to be pots and pans is an ignorance of their original purpose. Percussion instruments are created to make music, not chicken soup!

I said all of that to say this: many born-again believers are only making "chicken soup" in the Kingdom of God. They could be doing what they were originally created to do by blending into God's symphony of dominion over Satan's kingdom of darkness! But all too often, the only thing we hear around the church are the clinks and clacks of some believers as they stir around in the soup of their own unbelief. Their unsynchronized beatings blare out as contrary speaking to the plan of God's dominion over Satan in their life. Remember, imaginations run wild when the ignorance of purpose abounds in life.

So learn to shut off the negative voices of defeat. And remember, it doesn't matter who you are, what race or what your past defeats, problems, or even personal victories are. When you are born again, you both die and come alive again at the same time. You die to the unregenerated physical person you once were and come alive as a person born of God's Spirit. Along with this wonderful gift of new life comes the opportunity to begin living with a new personality — the personality of the Holy Spirit with power and victory. When you invite the Holy Spirit into your life, you allow the personality of God to be seen in all you do. The Lord will empower you to overcome in every situation. And He will do it through His power in you.

The Holy Spirit Is a Person, Not a Tongue

How the Acts 2:4 promise of speaking in other tongues ever became such a heated issue in the church is beyond biblical reason. The simple truth of the matter is, if you are a Christian, the Holy Spirit wants to operate and talk through you on this earth. Sometimes He speaks in English. Sometimes He does not. Sometimes He counsels. Other times He works miracles. This is wonderful because it provides you with the opportunity of working with God. It can be a disadvantage to the Lord because of His dependence on human cooperation to complete His vision, but it is a great advantage to you.

As we understand it in Trinitarian thought, God the Father is resident on the throne in heaven. God the Son resides at the right hand of the Father. But God the Holy Spirit is on earth doing the Father's work through believers who will receive Him through Jesus Christ. He wants to live in human beings — that's His place of residence.

But never let the fact that the Holy Spirit is the third person of the Godhead, even let Him be thought of as third in rank. He is the presence of God who comes to live in you. Unlike man, the Holy Spirit, lacks a physical body through which to operate. This is one of the reasons you are so valuable to the Kingdom of God. You give Him a physical avenue through which to talk to and touch people. To operate in this physical realm, a person must have a physical body, and as you yield your body to the Lord, you become a co-laborer with Him.

Satan hates to see the authority of God at work in the life of His children, because when they receive the Holy Spirit, they instantly have the authority to destroy Satan's works.

...For this purpose the Son of God was manifested, that he might destroy the works of the devil.

1 John 3:8

"And I will pray the Father, and he shall give you another Comforter, that he may abide with you for ever" (John 14:16). When Jesus said this, He intended for men and women to never be without the comfort of the Holy Spirit. Jesus said that He would pray to the Father, and that He, the Father, would give His believers in Jesus another Comforter.

The word, *comforter*, in Greek is the word *parakletos* (Strong's #3875). It means, "one called along side to help."

14

In other words, Jesus was saying as He was preparing to leave His disciples, "I have to leave this place, but I will leave you with another Comforter. You won't be left comfortless. The Father is going to send another Comforter, just like Me."

The Greek word used for *another* — *allos* — means "another one exactly like Me, even though He will not be Me." So Jesus was saying, "I will pray that the Father will send another one called along your side, just like Me. He is here right now. And in the same manner as I did when I was physically resident on earth, the Comforter, the Holy Spirit, will heal the sick, raise the dead, work miracles alongside of you, and will feed thousands in and through you."

So Jesus wasn't referring in John 14:16 to another Comforter who was physically just like Him. He was referring to a Comforter who was spiritually as He was. And as Jesus told us, He is called the Holy Spirit — not the Holy Body.

It isn't the physical features of Christ that we need to pattern ourselves after. It is the spiritual likeness of the person of the Holy Spirit. It is He who will cause you to operate in His power against the designs of the enemy. Your physical features don't qualify you as a powerful person. Neither the devil or God are too impressed with your physical attributes. They merely establish you as a dwelling place in which the Holy Spirit can live and operate through. So allow your body to become a **living sacrifice,** according to Romans 12:1,2, so that you may become a residence for the power of God.

First John 4:4 says, "...greater is he that is in you, than he that is in the world." Remember, "He" is that person in you sent by God in Jesus' place, with the answer for your every need.

I thank God that for the many years I have had to develop a close relationship with the person of the Holy

Spirit. He desires to commune with you and help you, too. The more I get to know the Holy Spirit, the more I know I need Him every moment of every day. He is as real as any other person to me. This may sound strange to some people, but He is closer to me than my wife, and my wife and I have been very close for many years. There is so much more for all of us to know about the Holy Spirit. He directs you by an inner witness that speaks to your spirit in His soft voice. He wants to direct you. So learn to yield to His direction. He has the best plans for your life.

The Holy Spirit Will Talk, Listen and Hear

Think about this for a moment: if the Holy Spirit is a person, would God put a person who is deaf and mute inside of His people? One who can't hear or talk to you? Also consider, if He couldn't hear or talk to you, and He is the Comforter, what words could He say to comfort you and be as good a Comforter as Jesus was? The answer is, He couldn't. Therefore, He must be able to hear and talk — to hear and talk to you. The Holy Spirit hears and has the ability to speak, lead, guide, and direct you into all of God's truth for every area of your life. But He doesn't have a physical body. So He dwells in the body of a believer. This is God's chosen way. He has chosen to use a physical body like yours to complete His work.

If you have grieved the Holy Spirit by neglecting Him in the past, ask for God's forgiveness and start fellowshipping with Him again today. And always keep in mind that He lives in you, so make the decision to respond to Him. God's desire was to give the Holy Spirit to you so that you could be blessed with His gentle touch, conversation, direction, and spiritual comfort.

1

The Power in You

Because of the state of the world today, many Christians and non-Christians live in a state of powerlessness and hopelessness. The feelings and thoughts that accompany this condition don't come from God. In this book you will learn to overcome them with the prescriptions provided in the Bible — God's timeless Word.

> **Now unto him that is able to do exceeding abundantly above all that we ask or think, according to the power that worketh in us.**
>
> **Ephesians 3:20**

No matter how hopeless your situation may appear to be, as a Christian, you have a power dwelling inside of you Who is ready to go to work — the power of God's Holy Spirit Who works in you. But if your circumstances are saying, "If God is able to do exceeding abundantly above all that I ask or think, why isn't He doing it?" — I ask you to read that verse again paying particular attention to the last words, **according to the power that worketh in us** (you). If you are wondering why God hasn't answered your prayers, remember that in God's plan, it is imperative that we do our part so that He can do His!

God has already done something incredible for you: He has positioned His will in direct relationship to your faith-filled actions. And in so doing, He has, through the sacrifice of His Son Jesus on the cross, given you access to His divine power! If you say, "I am not going to do anything until God does something," you need to know that God's Word teaches that you have the ability to access God's power in order to change your circumstances. But you must choose to change your situation and the circumstances around you. You can accomplish this by rejecting mediocrity and unproductive living. God has given His power to you! So exercise your faith by believing in what He has already done and you will find yourself able to tap into His power for every situation.

If God's power is dormant in your life, this book will help you discover how to activate it! As you discover the power in you, God's power in your life, things around you will begin to change. Sickness, disease, oppression, poverty, prejudice and lack are nothing but a powerless part of the curse of the devil. With God you have the authority to overcome. And this authority to break the power of the enemy can apply to every area of life. Even those areas that may have held you and your family in bondage. God's power in you will bring deliverance.

You are someone very special. God placed you on earth with an important purpose. So get ready to use the power God has placed within you to change the world around you as you discover your purpose and learn how to fulfill it.

The God-Given Authority

Luke 10:19 says, "Behold, I give unto you power to tread on serpents and scorpions, and over all the power of the enemy: and nothing shall by any means hurt you." The Greek word *exousia* (Strong's #1849) is used in this scripture. It means, a privilege, force, capacity, competency, freedom, mastery, or delegated influence. It can also mean, to receive authority, jurisdiction, liberty, power, right, and strength.

Luke 10:19 is not referring to snakes and little creeping things in the natural, but to the devil, who is called a serpent, the dragon, the adversary and the enemy. This means you can have a God-given authority through the power of God in you to tread on the works of the devil, his kingdom of darkness, and all of his demonic authority.

But, unless you use this authority, the world around you will never change in a positive way. As a believer, you have God's authority through His Spirit to change situations and circumstances without waiting for permission from the enemy. This is an authority the world doesn't have. Remember, (though they may not know it) the world around you is waiting for believers to use their God-given authority to change things for the better all around them. Without this, the world will continue in its hopeless condition. So believers like you must stand up to allow God to take control through you spiritually, with the power and authority God has given you.

Have you ever bought new tires for your car? Most customers buy only certain tires because of their tread design. And there is a reason they do this; they know the type of terrain on which they plan to drive. The salesperson at the tire store will say, "This tire has an all-weather, all-season tread for summer and winter." Or, "These are snow tires." The tires may have studs of steel pumped into the tread so they can grip the snow and pull you through. You can't successfully drive on bald tires in the snow. You must have tread hitting the road. And when you drive, the tires leave their mark in the road.

To strike a parallel, to get to where you are going in your Christian life, you must leave an impression, a pattern, a certain change in the world as you pass by. God wouldn't command you to tread on the enemy if He thought you didn't have the equipment to do it. He has provided you with the proper equipment, and you are now being trained to use it. As you learn to do the things of God, you can have the "tire" with the proper tread with the power to drive right over the devil.

In fact, anything you need to defeat Satan is already in your possession; all you need to do is decide to take action. If you are feeling fearful inside and think, "He's too big," just remember he is not! Stop over-promoting the devil! Remember, "...God has not given us the spirit of fear; but of power, and of love, and of a sound mind" (2 Timothy 1:7). Stand up and take the authority God has given you.

To take authority over the devil requires a vision past all fear. Don't just stand there gazing into heaven waiting for Jesus to come floating down to earth to give you the victory. You received your victory at the cross, and He is coming again soon. But in the meantime, we must use the authority He has given us until He returns. Jesus said you could do this with His help. So now is the time to release the power of God to let Him work in you. Don't wait until His return to operate in the authority He has already given you as a citizen of God's Kingdom.

It is time to get out of the comfort zone of defeat. It is comfortable because there is no work in defeat. All you have to do is sit still and accept it, perhaps complain about it a little, and kick back to enjoy it. For some people defeat is fun! Let's read Luke 10:19 again, "Behold, I give unto you power to tread on serpents and scorpions, and over all the power of the enemy: and nothing shall by any means hurt you." Again, one way to look at this Scripture is, "...serpents and scorpions, *the devil and his demons*, and over all the power of the enemy." If you are able to tread over all the power of the enemy, meaning there is no power over which you can't tread, then there is nothing left for you to fear. With this in mind, the following is a great suggestion: take the word *"can't"* and throw it out of your vocabulary. The only one impressed by your negative confession when saying what you *can't* do is the devil. God is interested that you know what you can do through Him.

It is important to understand the words "...and over all the power of the enemy...." The enemy — Satan and his demons — were given some authority, but, it is delegated authority, and only up to a certain rank. The authority you have inherited has been delegated to you from the same God, but at a greater rank — above the enemy's authority. Again, the word *power* in this Scripture is the Greek word *exuosia* (Strong's #1849) and means that you have been given the ability, privilege, force, capacity, delegated influence, authority, jurisdiction, liberty, power, right, and strength to tread on Satan's works!

Look at it this way, in the military, there are lieutenants and there are captains. A captain has authority over a lieutenant even though the lieutenant has some rank over his subordinates. According to the laws regulating any branch of the Service, this is the way it goes. Everyone who is connected with the military understands and must obey this chain of command. That's just the way it is. The lieutenants can argue it all the way to the highest court, but the procedure will stand. Any judge will tell you that a captain has authority, or rank, over a lieutenant within the guidelines of military law.

With this in mind, here is the good news! Jesus has ranked you as a captain, and the devil is only a lieutenant! Satan was delegated *some* authority, but you have inherited *all* authority through the price Jesus paid on the cross. This is why the Bible says you will tread over all of the enemy's power. And this is to be done without apology or fear. So no matter how much power the devil seems to have, you can tread over him because God's Word says you can.

As a believer, this revelation needs to become a part of your life. There is no reason the devil should run over your family, home, career, ministry, marriage, finances or any other area of your life. If he is doing so, it is because you are allowing him to have control. People are sometimes shocked when I tell them that allowing the devil to have power over them is in disobedience to God. They don't realize God's authority has been given to them as a believer, and that God has been ready for Christians to take control of their authority for two thousand years. So you have no reason, as a captain in God's army, to allow a lower-ranking lieutenant from the enemy's army to dominate you and tell you what you can or can't do. He has no authority over you according to the Law of the universe — the Word of God.

When facing a problem, many Christians say, "I better find someone who has enough authority to help me." This is like an on-duty, uniformed police officer running to a phone booth to dial 911 when he encounters a criminal. He has been given the authority to face criminals, but instead he calls in fear, saying, "Quick! Send the police!" The problem is, when he dials the phone, it rings at his own home. As a believer in Christ, you are to serve as the spiritual police enforcing the will of God against any violations of His Word by the devil and his demons. You are that someone God has been looking for! The authority has been given to you through the power in you, the power of God's Holy Spirit.

I believe many Christians haven't understood how to utilize God's power because they haven't had to pay the high price that Jesus did for it. But Jesus paid the price, and we now have access to all He paid for. Many act as though they don't deserve or aren't worthy to receive the power of God. They think they have to suffer in order to receive from Him and don't realize that the power of God is available to all who believe. Just ask, and receive. He is waiting for you to use the power He has given you.

As a born-again believer, you can ask God for the gift of the Holy Spirit. You have been converted by His Spirit, so now you are ready to be filled with Him. Luke 11:13 says,

"If ye then, being evil, know how to give good gifts unto your children: how much more shall your heavenly Father give the Holy Spirit [the power] to them that ask him?" When you receive the gift, the Holy Spirit brings with Him an evidence of His power. You will begin to speak in another tongue as it is explained in Acts 2:4; Acts 10:44-46, and 1 Corinthians 14. Once this evidence begins to operate in your life, start using your new gift to charge yourself spiritually, daily, according to Jude 20:

> But ye, beloved, building up yourselves on your most holy faith, praying in the Holy Ghost.

As you do this, you will break through the restraints that had previously held you back from receiving God's blessings and victory.

According to Proverbs 18:21, "Death and life are in the power of the tongue: and they that love it shall eat the fruit thereof." This Scripture indicates how important it is to stop empowering the enemy with your mouth! We give the devil power if we go around saying, "Oh, you don't know what the devil has done to me today." Or, "I would have been successful, but the devil stopped me." I am glad the devil didn't stop Jesus when He was on the cross and was resurrected from the grave. Do yourself and the Kingdom of God a favor and don't promote the devil's abilities. Instead, bind him, cast down his imaginations and suggestions, get him out of the way — and move on.

Do you realize that the word, *over,* is the opposite of the word, *under?* You have been given power *over* the devil. Believers are in the best possible position: they are on top — the devil is *under.* He is under, or below, you. Some people say, "But the devil may hurt me. You don't want to talk about the devil because he will get mad and hurt your children." If you are worried about what the devil can do, read Luke 10:19, "...and nothing shall by any means hurt you." For the devil to hurt you, he must be given free reign to do so. So don't empower him, resist him! According to James 4:7-10:

> Submit yourselves therefore to God. Resist the devil, and he will flee from you. Draw nigh to God, and he will draw nigh to you. Cleanse your hands, ye sinners; and purify your hearts, ye double minded. Be afflicted, and mourn, and weep: let your laughter be turned to mourning, and your joy to heaviness. Humble yourselves in the sight of the Lord, and he shall lift you up.

You have been given authority over Satan's power. So thank God that He Himself is the One Who lifts you up!

Never forget that the devil has already been defeated. Therefore, when you fight him, you are fighting a loser. He has been stripped of his rank, and there is nothing you can do to defeat an enemy that has already lost except remind him of his defeat — with God's Word. If you were taught that you are suffering for the Lord with sickness in order to defeat the devil, remember, the Bible doesn't say that. God doesn't want you to live in sickness. He has already defeated the devil and has planned a victorious life for you. Jeremiah 29:11 says:

> For I know the thoughts that I think toward you, saith the Lord, thoughts of peace, and not of evil, to give you an expected end.

The Power of the Word

In Genesis 1, the Lord shows us how faith works through His Word:

> In the beginning God created the heaven and the earth. And the earth was without form, and void; and darkness was upon the face of the deep. And the Spirit of God moved upon the face of the waters. And God said, Let there be light: and there was light.
>
> **Genesis 1:1-3**

God spoke the world into existence knowing that what He spoke would come about. He spoke those words in faith. Still, for some Christians the power of God never seems to operate in their lives. They have been taught to trust in unbelief rather than God's Word. And they don't realize that the Spirit of God is ready to work through them on their behalf. Other Christians have been taught to find excuses. They feel they must constantly apologize for what has (or has not) been going on in their lives. Then when someone around them talks about faith and power, they close their eyes and ears.

I attended a church during my early Christian years that believed God wasn't capable of doing much on their behalf. In fact, people in our church used to laugh at my wife and me for visiting crusade meetings that taught about faith, healing, and the power of God. Maybe you have had a similar experience. If you have, don't be discouraged, Jesus was also mocked. Many religious men told Him that He was healing people through the power of the devil.

The Power in You

God's desire is for His covenant sons and daughters to operate in the same power that Jesus operated in while He was on earth. God has given you His power, but if that power has been dormant in you, I want to encourage you to stir His power up! This is what Paul encouraged Timothy to do, as I now encourage you.

> **Wherefore I put thee in remembrance that thou stir up the gift of God, which is in thee by the putting on of my hands.**
>
> **2 Timothy 1:6**

Having the fullness of God's Spirit doesn't mean that you will never experience personal problems or that you won't have to deal with adverse circumstances. What it does mean is that the power of God, that is full within you, will be able to help you deal with those situations. When you live in total obedience to the Lord, you allow His blessings to flow freely into your life. He wants you to live in victory, not in agony.

Many well-meaning Christians have been taught to believe that it is hard to get God to come down from His throne to help them. They believe it is all up to God and that they don't need to do anything in order to change their circumstances. They think God is just too busy to make any moves on their behalf. Some people have even been taught that God is unpredictable and finicky, and that He doesn't want to help them. Others feel God is prejudiced against them for whatever reason. They feel He disregards them because of their race, color, family background, economic status, past sins or their lack of calling. So they say to themselves, "You never know what God will do."

God Is Not Too Busy for You!

But I want you to know that God is not too busy for you and that He is certainly not fickle, finicky or prejudiced against you. God has given you His power to work through all your circumstances in life. The problem is that some Christians aren't knowledgeable of God's Word. They simply don't realize that Jesus is "...the same yesterday, to day, and for ever" (Hebrews 13:8). And they don't understand that all the deeds Jesus did while He was on earth, He has empowered His children to do.

I believe that many Christians, especially ministers, are working themselves entirely too hard. God isn't looking for you to *work* for the power in you; His power in you is there to do His work. You need to associate the word *power* with the Spirit of God, not with the religious works of the flesh. Many people find themselves trying to *do* something for the Lord. But that is not the proper position. The position should be, "God is doing something, so let me work with what He is doing." It is the Spirit of God Who works in you toward fulfilling God's ultimate vision for your life.

26

If you have been working too hard, maybe you have been working alone, because God is not doing what you desire to do for Him. That is not what God intended for you. He wants to have a father and son relationship with you. In such relationships, the son works with the father. My son, Donald Shorter, Jr., who is seven years old, is a great helper. He wants to help me do anything I am doing, even if he doesn't know how. He simply watches me do what I am doing, then duplicates my actions without questioning them. Even when he has no idea of what I am doing, he happily tries to help me. When you become born again, you become a son or daughter of God and He becomes your heavenly Father. So it is important that you find out specifically what He has for you to do, then do it. God will always empower the work that He is doing with you. And He will always do it through the power in you.

There are many powerless Christians who expect God to empower them to do what *they* want to do. And of course, much of the time what *they* want to do is contrary to what *He* wants. It is God's power, according to His will, that does the work, and you can't work it up. If you will let Him, the power of God working in you will fulfill His vision for every area of your life.

So begin to give free reign to the power of God — including the area of your thought life. Unbelief will only hinder God's ability to work on your behalf. "[He] is able to do exceeding abundantly above all that we ask or think...." Don't restrict God's power through shallow asking and thinking. Proverbs 23:7 says, "For as he thinketh in his heart, so is he: Eat and drink, saith he to thee; but his heart is not with thee."

Ungodly Thinking and Lifestyles That Hinder the Power of God

In my book, *Casting Down Imaginations*, I outline a complete five-step process of overcoming thought obstacles through faith in the Word of God. The process is based on 2 Corinthians 10:4,5 which says,

> For the weapons of our warfare are not carnal, but mighty through God to the pulling down of strong holds; casting down imaginations, and every high thing that exalteth itself against the knowledge of God, and bringing into captivity every thought to the obedience of Christ.

These verses teach how to break down the mental *"thought castles"* that may be hindering the power of God from operating through you.

Lifestyle is another aspect that can encumber the power of God in a person's life. During my years as a pastor, I have often seen people living a lifestyle of lies, while they regularly attend church. For example, one couple that started attending church where I pastor came to me one day and introduced themselves by saying they were married. Yet, they weren't, and had never been. In fact, the man was married to another woman who lived in another state, and had deserted his wife and two children for this adulterous affair. The adulteress he was currently living with had three children by him. They were living a lie.

The power of God won't work through a lying vessel who is committing adultery, or any other sin that is willfully and consistently lived out. The Bible states clearly in Luke 12:2,3:

> For there is nothing covered, that shall not be revealed; neither hid, that shall not be known. Therefore whatsoever ye have spoken in darkness shall be heard in the light; and that which ye have spoken in the ear in closets shall be proclaimed upon the house - tops.

To think that God could empower and bless this kind of lifestyle is an insult to Him. This is an awesome thought, but we can actually grieve (torment), the Holy Spirit of God with our actions. And this is only one example of the sort of thing that will hinder the power of God from operating effectively.

I met another couple years ago who had just opened a small Christian bookstore. They advertised on the Christian radio station that my wife and I owned. The entire time we did business with them, they always paid for their advertising in cash, and expressed a strong love for God. But, as time went by I would hear them complain about how God was not providing for their needs. Occasionally, I would even hear the husband release his anger toward God because of one thing or another.

Then one day, as he was paying for his advertising, this man mentioned he would be closing the bookstore. When I asked why he said, "I will be moving very soon because they have found me again." His explanation shocked me, but it helped me understand my perplexity over their business practices, complaints, and the lack of God's power in his ministry.

As it turned out, this man and his new wife were on the run from the child support obligations he had from his previous marriage. Because of this, he always dealt in cash and rarely exposed his identity or social security number. To keep the authorities from finding him, whenever they got close, he would move to another city. And he planned to live this way for the next six to eight years until the children from his previous marriage had grown past the age for child support.

This Christian bookstore owner's actions were irresponsible and unscriptural, and give Christians, in general, a bad name. There was no power in his life, and who could wonder why? God is no respecter of persons. Sin will hinder His power from effectively operating in anyone's life. First Timothy 5:24,25 says,

29

> Some men's sins are open beforehand, going before
> to judgment; and some men they follow after. Likewise
> also the good works of some are manifest beforehand;
> and they that are otherwise cannot be hid.

For some people, God's mercy can even lead to their downfall. God doesn't always settle His accounts at the end of each month. Eventually, every person will pay for what they have done. For many Christians, payday has already begun in the form of a lack of God's power, and their embarrassment in front of the world. Sin is not a doctrine or teaching. It is a diabolical ruination of anything that is good. Romans 6:23 says, "...the wages of sin is death; but the gift of God is eternal life through Jesus Christ our Lord." It is you who will always determine what type of lifestyle that you live. God has left that decision up to you, and whatever you sow you will reap. Good or bad, the seed will eventually produce its fruit.

This was the case with the Christian bookstore owner. He knew that what he was doing was wrong. He tried again and again to receive the blessings and power of God and was continually frustrated. This man was also a pastor, so his sin affected his congregation as well. Every time he moved away he would leave behind a group of equally frustrated followers. Still, he refused to believe that his lifestyle had anything to do with the lack of God's power in his life. He was deluded and was completely oblivious to the fact that his ungodly practices were the reason for his powerlessness.

You Are Your Biggest Enemy

God is able to do greater things than we could ever think or ask, and the only person who can stop Him is you. The *devil can't stop God* from operating within us, and God won't, but your lifestyle can. Only you and I can disable the power of God in our lives. No higher price could have been paid to get God's power in you. Jesus died to open the way to live in you. So in other words, it is you who becomes your biggest enemy as you work against God's plan for you.

Ask yourself right now whether or not God's power is working in you. If the answer is no, be encouraged in knowing that God wants His power working in you. He wants to help you overcome every opposing force and ungodly lifestyle habit that you can imagine. But you must choose to let Him. The Word of God and His power in you can gain dominion over every situation in your life. This will happen only when you choose to exalt the Word and develop a relationship with God through His Holy Spirit by faith.

Be Honest With Yourself

So be honest with yourself. Either the power of God is working in you, or it isn't. If God's *dunamis* power has been quenched through your choices in life, decide now to make changes that give Him free reign within you. Ask yourself whether you are hindering or enabling God to do what He wants to do through you today. When you allow the Lord to work in you, you allow yourself to become a person who is full of God's power. That is what *powerful* means: *full of power*. Let the power of God in you make you a powerful Christian. Allow God's Holy Spirit to move and do God's work in and through you.

2
The Power of God Gives You Victory

Some believers forget that as God's children, they have His promise of abundant blessings. So when they encounter difficult circumstances, they tend to focus on the situations and on their own inabilities instead of the ability of God. The fact of the matter is, as Christians, we are unable to do anything by our own power. But if we rely on Him, "He is able to do exceeding abundantly above all that we ask or think, according to the power that worketh in us" (Ephesians 3:20).

If you want to see what God can do, look around at His marvelous creation, then be encouraged! He wants to do something very exciting with you. To get involved in God's vision for you will bring an excitement into your life that is above anything you could imagine, ask or think.

What Are You Really Asking From God?

Are you living victoriously? Are you trusting God to receive His very best for your life? Be truthful — what are you really asking from God? What are you thinking and believing will happen? If you are asking God to help you just barely get by, you are receiving far less than what He is wanting to do. But if you are asking Him for more, make sure you ask in faith. James 1:6-8 says,

> But let him ask (of God) in faith, nothing wavering.
> For he that wavereth is like a wave of the sea driven
> with the wind and tossed. For let not that man think

that he shall receive any thing of the Lord. **A double minded man is unstable in all his ways.**

Make sure you aren't saying one thing, thinking another, and believing differently in your heart. Some people's mouth, mind and heart are in such disagreement with one another, that there is no place at all for God's Word. This kind of confusion guarantees nothing. The kind of unwavering faith that James is talking about believes and depends upon God's promises, regardless of circumstances. Remember, the power of God works in you through agreement with His Word. When you confess what you believe in His Word, the power of God will operate in you.

As a Christian you need to discipline your soul (mind, will and emotions) in order to live a victorious life in the midst of negative circumstances. So train your mind to rely on God's Word, and meditate upon it in your heart. As you do this, you will begin to live by faith and not by sight.

By Faith

The world is in desperate need of hope and change. And as Christians, we have the responsibility to bring them both through the power of God. The world is tired of hearing empty talk. They need to see a demonstration of God's power. But if we, the church, aren't living by faith, how can we be the example the world needs to see? The world will only be influenced by what they see in our lives. And if we don't reflect what we believe, we are like a company that tells its clients, "Don't talk to our salespeople about our product because they don't really believe in it."

The world deserves to see someone who accurately represents and demonstrates the authority of God. As it was in the book of Acts, they are waiting to see God's powerful Church. So we as believers should be confident in giving them the goods. We should be confident when saying, "This is part of what you will see happen in your life when Jesus becomes your Lord." The world has a right to know that we are the powerful body of Christ!

Is God's Power (Operating) in You?

Though no one has completely learned to trust God in every area of his or her life, there should be victory in many areas. The world should be able to say, "Look at that Christian's life. God is victorious in him. How does he do it? Perhaps he can help me." Take one area of your life at a time. And get started now by making a list of the areas in your life that you want to be a success. Dwell upon Christ's victory and cast down thoughts of defeat.

In order to live victoriously, the power of God has to operate effectively in three important areas of your life:

1. You must have a strong relationship with God.

Many Christians do things religiously or habitually without thought, study or reason. They don't do things from a scriptural standpoint, and this is very dangerous. Peer pressure doesn't stop at age eighteen. It continues on to the grave. Even in the Church, "Christian peer pressure" can rob Christians of the lifestyle that God has planned for them. The opinions of others often easily convince us to settle for a lesser God. A God Who "quit" manifesting His power and blessing. So let God's Word stand as the highest standard in your life. Base your actions on His Word, not on the false gods or the religious opinions of others. False gods often masquerade as so-called spiritual friends and even religious mentors who advocate old traditions or religious ways of doing things. And always be careful to check the motivation of *why* you are doing what you are doing in accordance with God's Word.

2. Submit to godly teaching.

The Body of Christ is in need of godly teaching. During His ministry on earth, Jesus went about preaching, *teaching* and healing. Before He returned to the Father, He appointed many others to continue teaching what He had taught them. So it is important to have the influence of a biblically based teacher. This means a man or woman who has been anointed and appointed by God to teach His Word in an accurate, understandable manner. The traditions of a denomination or an organization simply can't help. You need the anointed Word of God in your life. In doing and saying things out of religious creed and tradition, you may mean well, but it can be powerless. Many people think repetitiously, both good and bad, but this doesn't make them spiritual. Jesus addressed this sort of thinking in Mark 7:13,14:

> Making the word of God of none effect through your tradition, which ye have delivered: and many such like things do ye. And when he had called all the people unto him, he said unto them, Hearken unto me every one of you, and understand.

God wants you to not only hear His Word, He wants you to understand it. To hear and presume, is not to hear and obey. Religious repetition can make the Word of God of no effect.

The devil has tried his best to break down the credibility of those responsible for delivering God's Word. Satan would like nothing better than to have people believe that God's men and women in ministry are people using fables to fool people for their own gain. And, that they are motivated by their own opinions. To do this, religion has always been one of his most effective deceptions. The devil constantly uses religious ideas to discredit God's men and women, and to discourage those in the Church from receiving the truth. There is power in God's Word, but only false pretense in religion. So submit yourself to a church that is teaching the Word of God in an understandable way. Then as you apply God's Word to your life, you will achieve success.

Maybe you aren't involved in a local church. Maybe you float from church to church because you like to visit different ministries without making a commitment to any one church. If this is you, this kind of Christian existence will cause you to be unstable and powerless. Unless you are *committed* to strong, consistent teaching you will never reach your full potential. Every born-again person has a responsibility to submit themselves to a pastor who teaches the Word of God consistently.

It is time to cast down rebellion, past hurts, resentments and negative experiences from past relationships that may be holding you back from receiving the powerful influence of God's teaching. So submit yourself to the Word of God. Ask God to direct you to a ministry in which you can commit. You will prosper when you are submitted to a ministry where the pastor and his leadership not only teach the Word of God in a powerful, understandable way, but also live out the biblical principles that they are called to teach.

3. **Be prepared to receive the law (the Word of God).**

Once you complete Step 2, you will be ready to prepare yourself to receive and accept God's unchangeable Word in your life. Don't accept it as a great idea that might work for some people, or as simply a good suggestion that could affect your life. Instead, accept it as the command of God by which you are to live. Commit yourself to trust in His Word. You will live life to the fullest as you learn to live by every word that proceeds from out of God's mouth.

A scriptural outline for Steps 1 and 2 is found in 2 Chronicles 15:1,2:

> **And the Spirit of God came upon Azariah the son of Oded: And he went out to meet Asa, and said unto him, Hear ye me, Asa, and all Judah and Benjamin; the Lord *is* with you, while ye be with him; and if ye seek him, he will be found of you; but if ye forsake him, he will forsake you.**

This sobering statement is still true. God is with you. He will never leave you or forsake you. But He won't force His way into your life. God is looking for people who will seek and obey Him, and He is seeking you. Wherever you may have already tried to run in the past, He was there. So when you give Him every area of your life, what you truly desire will be waiting for you. God is looking for people who are looking for Him.

The book of Chronicles adds to our outline, this time in verse 3:

> Now for a long season Israel *hath been* without the true God, and without a teaching priest, and without law.
>
> **2 Chronicles 15:3**

This passage shows that three things were missing in Israel:

1. The true God.

2. A teaching priest (a minister to teach God's Word).

3. And the Word of God (the Law).

Israel had been involved with other religious gods and had left the true God. Maybe you or someone you know is living the same way, ignorantly looking for someone or something to worship. Many people are sincere in their desire to worship God, but they lack the knowledge of how to worship properly. Then there are others who know some basics of "Deity" worship, but they don't know how to worship the true God in Spirit and in truth. They worship religiously as a matter of convenience by putting something or someone they call a god, and their own desires, first.

Any of this can and does happen in the Christian Church. Sincere Christians can be sincerely wrong in worshipping false gods. False gods are the gods of one's own making to serve selfish needs.

Again in the above passage, God's people were worshipping — but they weren't really worshipping the true God. They were missing the three key elements necessary for worship. And because of this, they were left powerless, hopeless and vexed with problems.

> **But when they in their trouble did turn unto the Lord God of Israel [or, when they were in a pickle], and sought him, he was found of them. And In those times *there was* no peace to him that went out, nor to him that came in, but great vexations *were* upon all the inhabitants of the countries.**
>
> **2 Chronicles 15:4,5**

God wanted His Old Testament people to be powerful men and women for Him. This is also His desire for you and me. But we need to understand that we can't use God as a parachute and only communicate with Him when our airplane of life is about to crash. After we pull our rip cord as we plummet to the ground, we always expect our parachute to catch in the wind, and to be rescued again! Then after God saves us, we thank Him and treat Him as if He were our own personal rescue team, or our butler on call.

But God won't play the butler game very long. Samson proved this. The Spirit of God was on him. He had a covenant with God that only he and his parents knew about. His powerful physical strength was contingent upon his covenant that was bonded by a vow that he would never cut his hair, or drink alcoholic beverages.

In turn, God would provide Samson with supernatural physical strength to always defeat his enemies. He could simply shake himself, and the power of God would come on him. It didn't matter how many weapons or men came against him, the strength of Samson's covenant would make mincemeat of them.

Once he knocked out an entire army with the jawbone of an ass, but he abused God's power in this famous

39

instance for his own revenge. This wasn't God's design for the use of His power. The covenant between Samson and God was based on Samson's relationship with God. And Samson made many other mistakes.

Exchanging Relationship for Ritual: Samson's Mistake

One mistake that Samson made, many believers make daily. He gradually replaced his strong covenant relationship with a weak, fleshly "ritual" to maintain God's power in his life. Many Christians fall into this very same rut every day. They praise God while at the same time separating themselves from their covenant and Word-centered relationship. And they do it, like Samson, without even realizing what is happening. False, empty worship of the flesh creeps in, replacing true covenant worship in the Spirit, which ultimately destroys the covenant.

Samson's supernatural power and strength were taken away because of his intimate times spent with the enemy's agent, Delilah. His message is really very simple: spend time cohabitating with the enemy, and he will take your power.

> **And she (Delilah) made him sleep upon her knees; and she called for a man, and she caused him to shave off the seven locks of his head; and she began to afflict him, and his strength went from him. And she said, The Philistines be upon thee, Samson. And he awoke out of his sleep, and said, I will go out as at other times before, and shake myself. And he wist not that the Lord was departed from him.**
>
> **Judges 16:19,20**

After an intense, deceitful investigation, Delilah discovered the secret of Samson's covenant — it was symbolized by his hair, which was never to be cut. So she plotted to violate this covenant by cutting his hair as he slept in her lap. She carried out her scheme, and his covenant was broken. And Samson, like so many defeated religious believers of today, never recognized that he himself had authorized the stripping of God's supernatural power from his life by breaking his own covenant. He assumed, as many have, that nothing would change, and he never really recognized that God's power had left him.

Ritual or Covenant? Where Are You Today?

Like Samson, many Christians attend church services every day, read the Word, pray, make confessions and go through the motions of worshipping God, expecting His power to remain intact. To them, serving God and going through a ritual to receive His blessings is just a service routine. But the consequence of this lifestyle is powerlessness in the believer's life. And like Samson, they don't even recognize it. In time this lifestyle will cause people to sit home, backslide and return to a sinful life.

Samson immediately suffered the consequences for living his sinful life. He was immediately bound and destroyed physically by his enemies. For some the process draws out over a number of years. And then, like Samson, they never recognize their spiritual breakdown until a physical manifestation appears.

Enemy Dominion Is Not in God's Plan for You!

Many Christians are living today under enemy domination. The devil and his forces dominate every area of their lives. If you are one of these Christians, the good news is, you can reverse the enemy's domination in your life. It is your choice as a Christian to stop operating in religious ritual and routine. It is your choice as a Christian to stop allowing the enemy to dominate your life. A strong commitment to God is what is needed. A renewed covenant will enhance your relationship with Him and will increase the operation of His power in your life.

No "Delilah" Surprises

The Bible says in John 16:13 that the Holy Spirit **will guide you into all truth.** This means that if you are in relationship with Him, there is not much the enemy can do to surprise you. Samson lost the power of God because of one foolish surprise by the enemy. Had his relationship with God been stronger, this never would have happened. So let's be careful not to fall into this trap.

Seven Steps to Victory

There are seven steps that you, as a Christian, can follow to allow the power of God to operate in your life. I offer them now as a plan of attack to begin the process of change in your personal and family life.

1. Take courage now. No matter what you are facing, don't be afraid. Fear is an enemy!

As a believer in Jesus Christ, you have the ability to face any situation, because God has empowered you to change your circumstances. God's power and ability in you are ready to enable you to stand up against the devil. So don't make excuses. Take courage against the devil, **be bold** and you will win over every adverse circumstance.

2. Put away idols.

Put away the idols that you have permitted in your life. They could consist of secret sins, such as pornography, drugs, alcohol, the occult, witchcraft, rebellion, envy, bitterness, or strife.

3. Gather together with God's people regularly.

Assemble together with other believers regularly (Hebrews 10:25). Coming together with other Christians to receive the Word of God is essential to your spiritual growth. It is important for you to be a part of the corporate Body of Christ through a commitment to a church that has anointed Bible teaching. You may have to drive a few miles each week to receive this input into your life, but it is worth it.

4. Be ready to give what you have received.

Be ready to give of yourself, your talents, gifts, finances and love. This can only happen if you are regularly receiving from God's Word. Many people are bored with the Christian lifestyle because they aren't sharing what they have already received. Christians who lack a vision to give to others will be bored, powerless and frustrated. Your life will be fulfilled as you give and receive, just as Jesus did.

5. Develop a lifelong vision of commitment to Christ.

My wife and I have developed a long-range vision for our lives together. We have also developed a mutual commitment to the Lord. In fact, we have found that making and keeping commitments together can be fun. Everyone is looking for a purpose to which they can commit, so why not commit to the God of the universe? Some people put a couple of weeks into a commitment to God, then go back to the world because they didn't see others with strong commitments. God will only trust you with His power once you make life-changing, long-term commitments to Him.

6. Stick to your commitment to God.

Don't let go of your commitment. The Body of Christ needs people with strong commitment. Over 50 percent of all marriages, even of those in the Church, end in divorce. This is an obvious sign that the commitment of covenant is on the decline. Commitment can become one of your greatest attributes. So make a decision to remain committed in spite of circumstances or feelings.

> Take heed unto thyself, and unto the doctrine (the
> Word); continue in them: for in doing this thou shalt
> both save thyself, and them that hear thee.
>
> 1 Timothy 4:16

7. Learn to praise God.

Praise releases the Christian's faith in God and in His
promises. Great things will begin to take place when you
express your belief in God. Actions, based on faith, please
God, because He is a God of faith. So learn to praise Him
with faith in your heart. God's Word has already told you
what He will do for those who love Him.

King Asa's Seven Steps

Now let's read 2 Chronicles 15:5,6,8-15 to see that these
seven steps were the very steps that King Asa implemented
to restore God's kingdom in Judah. He applied them in
obedience according to God's prophesied Word:

> And in those times *there was* no peace to him that
> went out, nor to him that came in, but great vexations
> were upon all the inhabitants of the countries.
>
> And nation was destroyed of nation, and city of
> city: for God did vex them with all adversity.
>
> And when Asa heard these words, and the prophecy
> of Oded the prophet, *he took courage, and put away the
> abominable idols out of all the land* of Judah and
> Benjamin, and out of the cities which he had taken
> from mount Ephraim, *and renewed the altar of the Lord,*
> that was before the porch of the Lord.
>
> *And he gathered all Judah and Benjamin, and the
> strangers with them out of Ephraim and Manasseh, and
> out of Simeon:* for they fell to him out of Israel in
> abundance, when they saw that the Lord his God was
> with him.
>
> *So they gathered themselves together at Jerusalem in
> the third month,* in the fifteenth year of the reign of
> Asa.

And they offered unto the Lord the same time, of the spoil which they had brought, seven hundred oxen and seven thousand sheep.

And they entered into a covenant to seek the Lord God of their fathers with all their heart and with all their soul;

That *whosoever would not seek the Lord God of Israel should be put to death,* whether small or great, whether man or woman.

And they sware unto the Lord with a loud voice, and with shouting, and with trumpets, and with cornets.

And all Judah rejoiced at the oath: for they had sworn with all their heart, and sought him with their whole desire; and he was found of them: and the Lord gave them rest round about.

2 Chronicles 15:5,6,8-15

When Asa heard Oded's words, first, he (1) "took courage." Then he (2) "put away the abominable idols out of the land," and "renewed the altar." Next, he (3) "gathered with God's people," to (4) give what they had received by offering "the spoil which they had brought." Then they (5) "entered into a covenant to seek the Lord God," and agreed to stick to their covenant by decreeing (6) "whoever would not seek the Lord God of Israel should be put to death. Then finally, they praised the God of their renewed covenant with (7) "a loud voice and with shouting, and with trumpets and cornets." The fruit of Israel's actions was God's response of "rest round about them," in this passage's last verse.

God will release His power through you more and more as you put these seven simple steps into practice and begin to walk in them daily. As you do, you will be preparing yourself to be used by God in a greater way.

3

The Power of God in Financial Matters

It is He that giveth them power to get wealth....

You can believe in God's power in you to improve your financial matters too. Simply ask God to open your mind to the truths of His Word in this area. Then, as in all things, know that obedience to His Word will bring God's blessings.

> But thou shalt remember the Lord thy God: for it is he that giveth thee power to get wealth, that he may establish his covenant which he sware unto thy fathers, as it is this day.
>
> **Deuteronomy 8:18**

It is God Who gives you the power to get wealth. Notice that God doesn't say He will *give* it to you. He says He will give you the *power to obtain it.*

Some Christians think of the word *wealth* as a dirty word. They erroneously believe wealthy people are evil. Some Christians are even prejudiced against wealthy people and have been taught to avoid wealth because it will cause them to be evil. But if wealth was evil, why would God have given His people the ability to obtain it? The answer is, He gives us the power to become financially independent so that we never live in poverty. This means that no one — the government, prejudice, layoffs, lack of education or the economy — can control your finances. God is in control. And, it takes money to preach His gospel.

God has given you the power of financial freedom. He doesn't sell it to you; He gives it to anyone who will believe and receive it. This means that every believer has the ability to rise above poverty. It won't happen overnight, but with God's power, and faith in Him, it will happen.

Your Faith Is Your Wealth

Wealth represents more than money. It includes everything God has given you — His gifts, talents and abilities. The potential that is in you — your education, skills, career training and who you are in Christ — can all be used for the Body of Christ. But to receive God's power, your faith must play an active role. Your own wealth is based on your own faith in what God has said in His Word. It is you who must make the choice to live in poverty or to be prosperous and enjoy God's blessings.

> But thou shalt remember the Lord thy God: for it is he that giveth thee power to get wealth, that he may establish his covenant which he sware unto thy fathers, as it is this day.
>
> Deuteronomy 8:18

God desires His power to work in you, not just for your benefit, but for the benefit of others as well. You have been given the power to obtain wealth as a part of your covenant with Him. The covenant is the propagation of the Gospel.

As a born-again believer, you are not a powerless person. You are not stuck without the ability to change your circumstances. It doesn't matter whether you are a grandmother taking care of your grandchildren on government assistance, or a millionaire perplexed over making a multimillion-dollar decision within the next hour. Whoever you are, God has given you the power to obtain wealth by using His power that dwells within you.

The ability to change your destiny is within you, and God has a plan for you to go farther with Him. It is no longer up to you alone. You have the God of the universe on your side.

The Power To Defeat Stagnation

The power of God does not guarantee success, but properly using His power does. Believers all over the world have within themselves the power to change situations to line up with God's will. Still, many of them constantly ask, "God, why don't You change my situation?" They are God's people with His power, but that power lies dormant within them. They have the ability to change world situations, but they don't do their part.

In Exodus 14, the Israelites appeared to be trapped, facing the Red Sea. Some Christians believe God "carried" them through the sea bed, but He didn't. In fact, He had little to do with their going forward once He parted the waters.

Maybe you were one of those who were taught that God rushed the Israelites through the midst of that magnificent miracle, without any thought or effort on their part. But think about it, if they had waited for God to "push" them through, they surely would have perished. No, they had to do something for themselves, even though God gave Moses His power.

It was God's power that parted the Red Sea, but it was God's people who had to decide to walk through to victory! It took faith on their part to complete this great act of God's grace. They could have been defeated, as many Christians are today, stalled on the brink of a miracle, waiting to be pushed through. But they acted on what God had already done, moved on with Him, and were BLESSED. God gives you the necessary faith to act on what He has already done too, but you must learn how to use it.

Because of the obstacles and situations in your life, you may be saying, "God, help me. This is like the Red Sea. I have the Egyptian army advancing behind me, mountains on one side, the water in front of me, and I can't get through!" But God is saying, "Go forward! Lift up My Word and go forward!"

> And Moses said unto the people, Fear ye not, stand still, and see the salvation of the Lord, which he will shew to you to day: for the Egyptians whom ye have seen to day, ye shall see them again no more for ever.
>
> Exodus 14:13

Like the children of Israel, the Holy Spirit has been dealing with me to press ahead. He has said to me, "Why do you always sit around and complain when the enemy is coming after you? A boxer who has never fought hasn't had the opportunity to prove himself. He will only be known as a champion when he defeats one opponent after another. So get out there and fight!"

It is God's desire for Christians to defeat the enemy on every hand, but some just won't fight. They hold back in fear rather than step up to fight. They walk away from impending victory, and God never receives glory through their lives.

If you are a Christian, God is saying to you today, "I have placed My power in you. I will show you how to win this battle through the Spirit. I'm in your corner. So, come on now, size your opponent. Look at him through My eyes. What a spiritual wimp! Now get out there and throw that uppercut! Good, square on the chin. Okay now, back up and let Me take a look at him. Now, go back and punch again. We can do it. Step back, duck and swing again. He's dizzy, he's staggering around like the loser I made of him at the cross. Now, here we go one more time. Pow! He's down. He's out. Put your hands up and give Me the glory and the praise! I am the One Who gave you the power to receive the victory. It's you and Me and we make one!"

However, instead of fighting the enemy under God's direction, many Christians say, "The enemy is behind me.

The mountains are to my side. God, why did You bring me into this fight in the first place?" They simply don't realize that they were brought into the fight to defeat the enemy and reinforce the victory Jesus already won.

I am not talking about physical violence, but about spiritual militancy against the devil. He puts up a fight, and he will take the victory from you by default if you let him. Sometimes it is simply a word war. He will try to win against you by making sure you hear about his strength. So don't let his hyped words cause you to fear and pull back. Christians lose many battles this way. The power to win is in you, but if you don't stand up and fight against the enemy, *you* have chosen to lose! Your proper use of God's power will guarantee success.

When I was in junior high school, I used to wrestle. Wrestling is one of the hardest sports to compete in because you are going body to body against an adversary in your own weight class. You either win all or lose all by yourself. If you lose, you can't say, "Someone didn't block for me," or, "I didn't get the pass at the right time," like you could if you were playing a team sport.

As a Christian, you are involved in a wrestling match against the devil. But always remember that you are *not* alone. Because God's power within you will fight on your behalf, when the fight is over, you will be the one standing in victory while your adversary is out cold. God will fight with you, but you must choose to fight. He won't push you into the seabed, or into the ring. Just never forget to give God the glory once the devil is down and out.

Finally, my brethren, be strong in the Lord, and in the power of his might. Put on the whole armour of God, that ye may be able to stand against the wiles of the devil. For we wrestle not against flesh and blood, but against principalities, against powers, against the rulers of the darkness of this world, against spiritual

wickedness in high places. [Your fight is not physical, but spiritual.] Wherefore take unto you the whole armour of God, that ye may be able to withstand in the evil day, and having done all, to stand. Stand therefore....

Ephesians 6:10-14

God has given you the power to stand in the midst of the fight:

And Moses said unto the people, Fear ye not, stand still, and see the salvation of the Lord, which he will shew to you to day: for the Egyptians whom ye have seen to day, ye shall see them again no more for ever. The Lord shall fight for you, and ye shall hold your peace. And the Lord said unto Moses, Wherefore criest thou unto me? speak unto the children of Israel, that they go forward.

Exodus 14:13-15

So decide to go forward regardless of the circumstances, opinions, projections, fears or judgments that are against you. Determine to make some kind of progress toward the fulfillment of God's vision for your life. Then move forward to make progress toward God's victory every day.

Have you ever noticed that people enjoy discussing negative circumstances? They say things like, "I don't feel too good today. I feel down and out. Have you ever felt that way before?" Then someone else will respond, "Oh, yes, I have, and I almost died." With a little prompting comes a little more, "Bumps are going to come out on the side of your face and your tonsils will swell up. Then your eyes will become bloodshot and your face will turn blue. It's going to be terrible."

Though this may sound silly, it happens every day. It seems that we are always looking for someone to support our negative circumstances instead of looking to God's Word for support. We need to change our thinking. We need to find people who will agree with the good news of

God's Word. We need to find people who will help us go forward, not backwards.

The Lord told Moses to stir up His people to move past their fears. Like the Israelites, we need to realize that the power of God is in us, but unless we take action we will be defeated. So it is time to go forward!

Lifting Up the Standard of God's Word

But lift thou up thy rod [representing God's Word], and stretch out thine hand over the sea, and divide it: and the children of Israel shall go on dry ground through the midst of the sea.

Exodus 14:16

The rod in this scripture represents the command that God spoke directly to Moses. A rod was used by a shepherd to lead and protect. The rod that Moses used in the Old Testament can be symbolized in the New Testament as a sword. As Moses lifted it by faith at God's command, He participated in the parting of the Red Sea. It was also used in many other miracles as the Lord gave Moses command.

Like Moses, you can use God's double-edged sword to win against the enemy. Or, like so many among us, you can allow fear to stagnate you. Though there is a difference between the shepherd's rod and his staff, they are both used to lead. David said, "...thy rod and thy staff they comfort me" (Psalm 23:4). Therefore, they are both designed to bring comfort, not fear.

Many times a shepherd uses the hook on the end of his staff to gently pull the sheep in the right direction. Other times he may use it to comfort his flock by touching each individual sheep to let them know he is nearby in case of danger. This is how the Holy Spirit desires to operate in the believer's life. He is like the staff. The Word represents the unchanging rod, or the double-edged sword. So allow the Shepherd to lead you by His Word and by His Spirit in the

53

direction He has planned for your life, and know that His power is within you to take you across and to finish the fight.

4
Training To Defeat the Devil

One of the most important things we can ever do as believers is to sharpen our Word-action responses so we can react according to the Word of God rather than according to what we see. In order to have a powerful response to the challenges we face daily, we must feed our spirit with the Word of God.

Soldiers are drilled until they are trained to instinctively react to situations in a certain manner. In the same way you need to train yourself beyond your natural tendency to reason every situation out. Sometimes rationalizing a problem too long allows the subtle enemy to get into your thoughts. So it is important to learn to react with the Word of God — without concern for physical or personal consequence. Good soldiers are trained to react in this manner in the heat of battle. When you are in the heat of the battle is no time to finally break out your operations manual to learn how to fire your weapon. You had better know how to fire your weapon way before then! As a believer, your weapon is your Bible.

Actions and reactions must be based on what God's Word has taught you, not on old wives' tales, or the traditions of men. Professional soldiers have been trained to react to certain circumstances without thinking. Before they know what is happening, their body is already doing what they are supposed to do because of rigorous and repetitious training. In the same way, as God's Christian army, we should have this attitude always in our daily lives. We can learn to turn our circumstances over to the

Lord without giving too much thought to them. Opportunities arise every day. To learn is to hear; but to train is to do.

I have heard that the purpose of military alerts, or the mustering of troops to deploy for combat, are a regular exercise of military training. Whether it is an exercise or not is never known until they are ordered to deploy, or commanded to, "stand down."

The exercise helps to prepare for an enemy attack, and because of the experience, an army is even better prepared the next time around. Thousands of men may stand next to idling planes all night in full combat gear, then suddenly be told to go home. Or they could just as easily be commanded to board the planes, then fly into a combat zone.

Who is going to deliver you out of your situations? Jesus is, of course. So train yourself to rely on Him and to become reactionary to your challenges in accordance with His Word. Train yourself every day as those situations that conflict with God's promises arise, to believe God's Word anyway. Speak His Word, and act on your faith. The devil can only complete his attack if you buy his bluff. Again, Ephesians 3:20 says, "Now unto him that is able to do exceeding abundantly above all that we ask or think, according to the power that worketh in us." The word *power* in this verse is the same word used in Acts 1:8: "But ye shall receive *power*, after that the Holy Ghost is come upon you...." It is translated from the Greek word *dunamis* (Strong's #1411) which means "a force." So in Acts 1:8 God was talking about the fact that the disciples would have *His forceful power in them.* This is true for you, too, if you are a Christian. God's power can't be counteracted by any other force. It is a powerful, unstoppable force. In fact, the root of this word in the Greek translation means, "can do." This is an important reason why you should remove the word, *can't,* from your vocabulary. As a believer in Christ, you *can do* because of Christ Who is in you.

Facing the Challenges of Life

Casting all your care upon him; for he careth for you.

1 Peter 5:7

Because Christians are soldiers in God's army, the Lord has made provision for us to turn every challenge of life over to Him in the full assurance of His love and care. Some people play around with their problems, wasting time and perhaps even missing the Holy Spirit's perfect timing for solving them. They never move on to victory, because they get nervous and confused by what they see and hear. The Word says in Matthew 11:28, "Come unto me, all ye that labour and are heavy laden, and I will give you rest." This means that Jesus intends for us to have rest even in the middle of our trials. We can maintain a "rest" posture by looking to Him for the resolution of difficulties, instead of trying to work them out ourselves.

We can be trained to react quickly with the Word. It can be just as easy as learning our ABCs. Elementary school teachers use different methods to teach their students to remember them. They use songs, books, blocks and food. The idea is to use these audio and visual aids to make the letters become reactionary responses while children learn to form whole words. In the process, the ABCs become second nature to the word-structuring process. The Christian who has trained to make the process of problem-solving a second nature reaction has learned to treat life's problems in this way. How? When the enemy attacks, the Word of God is turned to immediately because that which is seen has been proven to be temporary through experience and faith in His Word.

While we look not at the things which are seen, but at the things which are not seen: for the things which are seen are temporal; but the things which are not seen are eternal.

2 Corinthians 4:18

Don't allow the cares of this world to encumber you from operating in the power of God. Many Christians allow cares, fears, worries and concerns about what other people might think about them to stop the flow of God's power through them. So when the cares of this world come, instead of taking on a man-pleasing attitude — retreat in prayer to examine the problem and receive an answer through faith and the Word of God. This doesn't mean that you close your eyes to the reality of life's problems. It simply means that you choose to believe God's Word instead, and cast your cares on Him. Learn to release your cares quickly to the best Caretaker — God.

As you cast those things you can't handle upon the Lord, you aren't evading life's responsibilities. You are doing what God's Word has invited you to do. So do what you can, then put the rest in God's hands. When we accept the truth that God created each of us for a specific purpose, we begin to realize that the things that come against us are meant to bring victory and growth into our lives. The Lord is faithful to perfect *everything* that concerns us (see Psalm 138:8).

5
Power To Be Vigilant

Be sober, be vigilant; because your adversary the
devil, as a roaring lion, walketh about, seeking whom
he may devour: Whom resist steadfast in the faith....

1 Peter 5:8,9

The Lord wants His children to be vigilant. In the above
passage, God's Word doesn't say the devil is a lion. It says
he operates as a roaring lion. First Peter 5:7-9 in *The
Amplified Bible* reads:

Casting the whole of your care — all your anxieties,
all your worries, all your concerns, once and for all —
on Him, for He cares for you affectionately, and cares
about you watchfully. Be well-balanced (temperate,
sober of mind, be vigilant and cautious at all times); for
that enemy of yours, the devil, roams around like a lion
roaring [in fierce hunger], seeking someone to seize
upon and devour. Withstand him....

If God says that we can resist the enemy, then He has
given us the ability to do just that. Why would God tell us
to withstand the devil if it wouldn't work? The devil can't
bring anything against us that God hasn't given us the
power and authority to overcome. So withstand him!

There is a devil, and he is after you. Some people
believe a loving God wouldn't create a devil. The truth is,
God didn't create the devil. God created Lucifer, and
Lucifer chose to become the devil (*diabolos*, "accuser,"
"slanderer," Vines p. 308), the enemy of God and man. He
used his free will to become a loser. He chose to rebel.

Confessing the truths of God's Word daily is an important part of keeping the devil in his place. As we boldly declare, "God's power that prevails over the enemy is working in me. The enemy can't affect me unless I allow him to do so," the enemy can't do anything to defeat us.

Jesus' Purpose

He that committeth sin is of the devil; for the devil sinneth from the beginning. For this purpose the Son of God was manifested, that he might *destroy the works of the devil.*

1 John 3:8

The Son of God was made visible and came to this earth in a physical body to destroy the works of the devil. As soldiers in His army, we are to uphold the victory He has already won. God has already destroyed the works of the devil in your life and He has given you power to dominate the devil. So look at what God did to the works of the devil in the past tense — not as something He will do someday. As Christians, we must discern the works of God.

For example, I have heard believers say, "I know that you went through a divorce, but it was for the glory of God." But if they were really discerning, instead they would say, "God wants the glory to come from putting your marriage back together! He gets no glory from the failure of your tearing apart!" Why would God want to get glory out of something He hates? He certainly doesn't hate the divorced person, but His Word says He hates divorce (Malachi 2:16). Therefore, God doesn't get glory from a divorce. The discerning Christian knows this.

I have also heard believers say, "I know that you have sickness and disease in your body, but through it, you can give glory to God." But God doesn't get glory from sickness and disease, because sickness and disease were removed by the power of God at Calvary. It is simply time to concur with Jesus' destruction of the devil's works in your life and to learn to discern the works of the devil from the works of God.

Think about this for a moment. Too many people run their lives according to the input of people around them. They say, "according to my professor," or "according to my mom," or "according to how I feel tomorrow," or according to "whatever else." We should live our lives according to what God has said in His Word and the power of God that is at work in us — nothing else! The apostle Peter writes,

> **According** (there's that word *according* again) **as his divine power hath** (past tense) **given unto us all things that pertain unto life and godliness, through the knowledge of him that hath called us to glory and virtue** (excellence).
>
> **2 Peter 1:3**

Therefore, to effectively operate in the power of God, you need to:

- Become familiar with the Word.

- Become intimately acquainted with the Spirit of God.

- Learn to use your faith.

I call these three foundational truths, the "elements" of God's power. They are, the WORD, the SPIRIT and FAITH.

Another foundational truth is PRAYER. Pray in the Spirit over every area of your life. Prayer in the Spirit will bring God's plan into place in your life.

> **Likewise the Spirit also helpeth our infirmities** (weaknesses): **for we know not what we should pray for as we ought: but the Spirit itself** (Himself) **maketh intercession for us with groanings which cannot be uttered. And he that searcheth the hearts knoweth what is the mind of the Spirit, because he maketh intercession for the saints according to the will of God. And we know that all things work together for good to**

them that love God, to them who are the called according to his purpose.

Romans 8:26-28

Praying in the Spirit allows you to pray God's perfect will for your life. It has always been God's plan to empower His children to have dominion. But it is only through the Holy Spirit that we can learn to place ourselves in that position.

God's idea of dominion is not arrogance. It is confidence. Jesus is described as both the Lion of Judah *(representing boldness)* and the Lamb of God *(representing humbleness and meekness, not weakness)*. This may seem a strange combination, but Christians need to have this same combination in their lives.

Confidence in Him

First John 5:14 says, "And this is the confidence [not arrogance] that we have in him...." Jesus will lead you so you can walk, talk, live, and operate with confidence and boldness.

With this kind of confidence working in you, you will see yourself as the best candidate in every area of life, because you are led by the Lord with access to His wisdom and power. You will see yourself as the best employee, politician, business owner, homemaker, parent, or minister because you have God's divine power leading you. As you learn to regulate your affairs, not only by the requirements of the laws of the land, but also by the requirements of the laws in God's Word, you will become more and more victorious. God's laws are higher than any law on this earth and carry with them supernatural power for the believer.

The Power of the Gospel

It is the Gospel in the Christian that gives us the power to dominate. Therefore, never be ashamed of the Gospel, because it is the power that will cause change in us to become the people God wants us to be.

Not long ago, the Spirit of God began to talk to me about an area of my life where I needed to make some changes. "You have to lose the weight. You are overweight," He said. Although I had improved my eating habits, I was 60 to 70 pounds overweight. I was born again at age twelve and filled with the Spirit at seventeen. I thought I had known the Lord for a long time, but it wasn't until just a few years ago that God began to deal with me about this area of my life.

I felt like the fat, jolly preacher. Then as the Spirit of God began to talk to me, I thought, "That's the devil. He's condemning me." But it wasn't the devil! The Holy Spirit is the One Who convicts of sin, and being overweight and neglecting my body was sin. I knew better, so I was being convicted by the Spirit of God. "You need to get some of that fat off. How are you going to preach three services each Sunday morning and travel? You're too fat." So I said, "Okay, God." Then He gave me two passages: 2 Corinthians 10:5 and 1 Corinthians 9:26,27. He gave me these scriptures, so I grabbed hold of them. I began to meditate on them and confess them, and I used them in a constant conversation with myself as to how I was going to behave around food.

> **Casting down imaginations, and every high thing that exalted itself against the knowledge of God, and *bringing into captivity every thought* to the obedience of Christ.**
>
> **2 Corinthians 10:5**
>
> **I therefore so run, not as uncertainly; so fight I, not as one that beateth the air: *But I keep under my body, and bring it into subjection*: lest that by any means, when I have preached to others, I myself should be a castaway.**
>
> **1 Corinthians 9:26,27**

These Scriptures really spoke to me. I took them personally and literally. Paul is saying, "I take care of my body. I have ownership of my body." He is talking as if he is standing outside of himself, saying, "That's my body over there. I take care of it."

Put another way, Paul is saying, "It is your spirit that must make the decision and say, 'I keep my body off of drugs. I keep my body away from alcohol. I keep my body off of apple pies. I keep my body away from sexual immorality, fornication and adultery. I keep my body under control.'"

These verses certainly fit with what God was saying to me: I keep my body under control. Notice, it says *keep*. It doesn't say *put*. *Keep* is a word of consistency. I don't just *put* my body under, I *keep* it under control consistently.

God is not only powerful enough to deliver you, He is able to keep you free. You can keep your body under control with His help. The power in the blood of Jesus can help you change all of your habits and adverse circumstances.

The Power To Take Authority

God's message to me was, "You have been called to the ministry, and you have to show that you can take control in this area, too. Take authority over every area of your life. You are designed to be in a position of dominion over sin and every other hindrance that comes from the devil." God's power is sufficient for you, too.

Destined To Rule

Then the word of the Lord came unto me, saying, Before I formed thee in the belly I knew thee; and before thou camest forth out of the womb I sanctified thee [or set thee apart], and I ordained thee a prophet unto the nations. Then said I, Ah, Lord God! behold, I cannot speak: for I am a child. But the Lord said unto me, Say not, I am a child: for thou shalt go to all that I shall send thee, and whatsoever I command thee thou shalt speak. Be not afraid of their faces: for I am with thee to deliver thee, saith the Lord. Then the Lord put forth his hand, and touched my mouth. And the Lord said unto me, Behold, I have put my words in thy mouth. See, I have this day set thee over the nations and over the kingdoms....

Jeremiah 1:4-10

Every believer has been destined to rule over the enemy. God has positioned us as people of dominion to be victorious in every situation in life. But maybe you have been told all your life that you were from the wrong side of the tracks, neglected as a child, or from a dysfunctional family. Or maybe you had no family at all. It really doesn't matter. Neither the tracks nor anything else have anything to do with what God has planned for you. Some single people say, "I'm just a single person. I can't do much." Or, "I have two kids, and I am a single parent." But remember, God is able! "I'm a single parent." God is able! "But, I'm a divorcee." God is able!

God's qualifications are centered on obedience to His Word. He is no respecter of persons. So stop disqualifying yourself. Some people say, "I didn't get all the education I need." So what! Use what you have until you are able to receive more. In the meantime, tap into God's wisdom, Word and power as an inexhaustible source of provision for whatever you lack.

In the following Scripture God says, "*I have set thee over.*" Take this truth as your personal position in life.

See, I have this day set thee over the nations and over the kingdoms, to root out, and to pull down, and to destroy, and to throw down, to build, and to plant.

Jeremiah 1:10

This is what you are called to do.

> Moreover the word of the Lord came unto me, saying, Jeremiah, what seest thou? And I said, I see a rod of an almond tree. Then said the Lord unto me, Thou hast well seen: for I will hasten my word to perform it.
>
> Jeremiah 1:11,12

God will *quickly* perform His Word for you. He won't perform what others say about you, or what they think about you, or how they look at you. What He will do is cause *His Word* to be performed in plain view for everyone around you to see. He will do it right before their eyes. This is His delight. So believe and receive God's promises, and He will fulfill your calling. The power of God *in you* is how He gets it *through you.*

Delighting Ourselves in the Lord

> Delight thyself also in the Lord; and he shall give thee the desires of thine heart.
>
> Psalm 37:4

A Vicious Cycle

To receive the fulfillment of God's promise in Psalm 37:4, learn to delight yourself in the Lord and to be obedient to His Word. This is difficult for some people because their focus is on past and present problems. They have a negative attitude, and their thoughts won't allow them to do what God's Word requires to receive from Him. Ultimately, their condition gets even worse because of consistently *living* in such unbelief. Some people are even mad at God because of the problems they face and believe erroneously that they are victims of some God-ordained plan for them to live a powerless life.

It is a vicious circle. Simply put, God wants us to delight in Him so we can receive the desires of our heart. It is time to do it and not just confess it. It is time to live His Word, not just memorize it.

God Has Ordered Your Steps

The steps of a good man are ordered by the Lord: and he delighteth in his way. Though he fall, he shall not be utterly cast down: for the Lord upholdeth him with his hand.

Psalm 37:23,24

Believing this Scripture, begin to confess: "God, You said that You would perform Your Word. So order the steps of my life. You said that I would not be utterly cast down and that You are upholding me with Your hand. So I praise You, Lord, for You are upholding me right now. And I thank You now for holding me up." And from now on in your life, always confess and pray according to the Word of God.

The power that God has placed in you will cause you to triumph over every challenge of life, so begin to enjoy all that God has given you. Delight yourself in Him and He will give you the desires of your heart. Prepare yourself to receive according to the power of His Word, His Spirit, and your faith. Remember 2 Corinthians 4:18:

While we look not at the things which are seen, but at the things which are not seen: for the things which are seen are temporal; but the things which are not seen are eternal.

This Scripture reminds us that as Christians on earth we deal with things that we can see which are only temporary. People all over the world are discouraged because they don't like what they see going on in their lives. Therefore, to be a success in life as a Christian, you need to begin to operate on what God's Word says.

As you live by God's Word, you will be able to bring hope to the hopeless. You will be able to see spiritually past what you can see in the natural.

6

Choosing Between the Spirit and the Flesh

When a person gets hold of the Word and mixes it with faith, victories in life become commonplace. Faith in God's Word allows His plans to be fulfilled in your life. But it only happens to those choosing God's Spirit over the whims of their flesh.

The Bible tells us of those in the synagogue who were astonished at Jesus' teachings. These religious Jews had *heard* the Word before, but they weren't accustomed to the kind of power and authority that Jesus walked in. What they were accustomed to were excuses and apologies.

> **And it came to pass on a certain day, as he was teaching, that there were Pharisees and doctors of the law sitting by, which were come out of every town of Galilee, and Judaea, and Jerusalem: and the power of the Lord was present to heal them.**
>
> **Luke 5:17**

Notice that this passage says that *the power of the Lord was present to heal them.* The power was present because Jesus was present. He was teaching God's Word — and He was God's Word. But that doesn't mean everyone there received His healing. Many religionists were there waiting to catch Him in an "unlawful" teaching or to see Him make an "unlawful" move. Some were simply there to watch. Many Christians perceive God in this way, without faith, in total flesh.

But there were many others present to receive from Christ's ministry who were hungry for God's Spirit. The Christian who approaches Jesus with this attitude is sure to receive God's many gifts. They are dispensed by His Spirit, unto those who are drawn by His Spirit to fellowship with Him.

It is the spirit that quickeneth (makes alive); **the flesh profiteth nothing: the words that I speak unto you, they are spirit** (power), **and they are life** (the God - kind of life).

John 6:63

The Holy Spirit will make alive whatever is dead. He gives life to dead marriages, families, careers, financial situations, ministries and people. As God's Word is believed in every area of life, every area of life can receive God's life from His Spirit.

The thief cometh not, but for to steal, and to kill, and to destroy: I am come that they might have life, and that they might have it more abundantly.

John 10:10

Zoe is the Greek word translated "life" in this verse. It means *the kind of life God has in Himself* (Vine's p. 767). So Jesus was saying, "I have come to give you God's kind of life — God's life in the Spirit — His meaning — His power. It is the Spirit that quickens, or makes alive. The flesh profits nothing. Whatever you are doing for your flesh will profit very little, but spiritual actions profit much" (author's paraphrase).

This means, you have to discipline your physical body. "You mean I can't just go out tonight and do whatever my physical body wants to do?" No, the power of God will not operate in you until you make a choice between the Spirit and the flesh — between life and death.

...the words that I speak unto you, they are spirit, and they are life.

John 6:63

When you make a decision for the Spirit, you make a decision for life, and a decision against the flesh and its death. But when you make a decision for the flesh and its death, you refuse the life of the Spirit.

Remember, God's Word and power bring life. His Word *is* life and gives you the power to change your life. So as you grow spiritually, take hold of the anointed Word of God — even if you can only comprehend one idea. Then use that idea to begin changing your life.

And never make light of anyone who is preaching or teaching the anointed Word of God. You may not like the way they look, or the way they preach. And you may only remember one key truth. But take that key truth and allow it to unlock your life. Then help unlock the lives of others around you.

7
Why Satan Fights

The enemy may pursue you for a season, but God will ultimately receive glory through the devil's defeat. Just remember that the enemy isn't only after you. He was mad at God long before you were born. God created you in His own likeness and image as a spirit being, and you represent God on this earth. As a born-again believer, you have a relationship with God that Satan lost because of rebellion and pride. He can't touch God, so he tries to touch you. And he will if he can manage it. But God has given you His power to continue Satan's defeat.

So keep in mind that God doesn't allow the enemy to come against you to overcome and defeat you. This would mean God would authorize His own defeat. God isn't glorified when His children are degraded and defeated. So if you are continuously defeated by the devil or by the negative circumstances of this world — drugs, alcohol, sexual passions, poverty, depression, fear, hate, prejudice, sickness, pain, emotional suffering, lack of self-esteem, lust of the eyes, lust of the flesh, or the pride of life — something is wrong. God isn't glorified when His born-again children are overcome by such base, carnal deceptions of Satan's fallen life. The Lord wants the glory through the devil's defeat as you fight and gain your victory over him.

The Hearts of the Egyptians

When God was preparing to deliver His people fr their Egyptian bondage, He said He would har Pharaoh's heart. And Pharaoh's army was working si side with the enemy. God could have moved the heart of this Egyptian king to call off his army. He could have moved him to say, "The Israelites are crossing the Red Sea, so just forget it. Why pursue them any longer?" But God hardened him to fully pursue them.

Why would God do this? Weren't things bad enough for the Israelites? Was God punishing them? The answer is written in Exodus 14. His Word says He did it for "honor."

> **And I, behold, I will harden the hearts of the Egyptians, and they shall follow them** (the Israelites): **and I will get me honour upon Pharaoh, and upon all his host, upon his chariots, and upon his horsemen.**
> **Exodus 14:17**

God wanted the honor and glory for winning His people's battle. Pharaoh was used of Satan to come against God's people. And remember, a battle must take place before there is a victory. In this one God chose to destroy Satan's army, powerfully — with a sea! Our battle as Christians was won 2,000 years ago through the death, burial and resurrection of Jesus Christ! Today the Lord wants us to fight the good fight of faith, upholding the victory He won for us. So don't run or be fearful. Instead, fight. Fight and you will win, because Jesus has already won!

> **And the Egyptians shall know that I am the Lord, when I have gotten me honour upon Pharaoh, upon his chariots, and upon his horsemen.**
> **Exodus 14:18**

When you are victorious over the challenges of life, people will know that God is your Deliverer, and He will receive honor. Maybe you have been moaning and complaining because you hear the enemy's chariot wheels behind you. But there is no need to complain or worry. God wants to deliver you! He will part your Red Sea! He wants make you victorious! So stop giving the enemy glory your words. The power to win every battle is already ing in you.

Paul reminded young Timothy that he, too, had something working in him that was very powerful.

When I call to remembrance the unfeigned faith that is in thee....

2 Timothy 1:5

Like Timothy, God's power in you is at work to make you different, distinct, and sincerely unique. So put faith in what God has already said. Faith *believes and speaks* God's Word. Faith in God gives us supernatural hope that completely overshadows the powerless and hopelessness of the world!

Stirring Up the Gift of God in You

Wherefore I put thee in remembrance that thou stir up the gift of God, which is in thee by the putting on of my hands.

2 Timothy 1:6

Like Timothy, we are to stir up the gifts with which God has blessed us. And as we do — because of the Holy Spirit who dwells within us — we can say to ourselves: "Wake up! I can change every situation around me that is robbing my life. I will allow God to use me as a vessel of His power, because His power is dwelling within me! The Holy Spirit will lead and guide me into miraculous victories. I don't have to live in mediocrity in any area of life, and I can help others out of the lifestyle of mediocrity and defeat. I don't have to live in stagnation, ruled by negative circumstances!"

Now, thank the Lord for giving you a revelation of the power He has placed in you!

My wife and I enjoy taking our family to the Washington coastline. During one of our many visits, my wife and children wanted to stay in the hotel, so I decided to rent a moped. I kicked it in gear and had a wonderful time riding on the beach next to the water to get a good view of the surf tumbling in. I was far away from everyone and anything except the seabirds, surf and sand.

On this outing I stopped in the gooey sand to pause and enjoy the ocean view for just a moment. I purposely left my moped engine running to avoid restarting problems. Then suddenly, the moped's engine stopped! In a panic, I remembered that the rental shop had experienced problems with it and nervously tried to remember their "emergency" kick-start lessons. So I pulled out the foot lever, put my foot on it as I had been shown, and pushed down as hard as I could. I did it over and over and over again, but nothing happened. The engine only sputtered. In fact, I kicked the foot lever so fast and hard that the moped had sunk deep into the sand, partially burying the wheels until I couldn't kick anymore.

Now the waves that were steadily crashing around and drenching me had turned what started out as an enjoyable afternoon ride, into an alarming tourist-nightmare. I kicked and sputtered and sunk even deeper — I had to make a choice. Push or sink. So I got off the bike, dug my feet into the goo, and pushed the thing back to the rental shop.

My moped experience always reminds me of how difficult it is to stir some people up. It's as though they want someone to jump on their back and kick their little starters in the ribs! As a pastor, I have been the "starter" many times. But after many attempts at jump-starting them, you want to say, "Forget it, you don't really want to get started anyway. So just sit there and drown in your self-pity and mediocrity!"

There comes a point when you have to allow people to jump-start themselves. They have a choice to make, and you can do only so much kicking.

When I finally got back to the rental shop, the manager gave me another moped. It was then that I learned an important bit of information for all moped riders. Mopeds come equipped with an automatic starter located on the handle bars. That's right, they can be started automatically! The power to start the engine is already in place. My moped had the ability to do automatically what I tried to do manually! It was equipped by the manufacturer to stir itself up. This is also true of every born-again believer. You were equipped the day you were born again to tap into the power of your own automatic starter — the power of God. His power is there, you simply need to know how to turn it on.

Building Yourself Up in Your Most Holy Faith

During my early years as a Christian, I was taught in my denomination to ask people to "pray my strength in the Lord." It was supposed to be a humbling, religious statement requesting prayer to "stay strong" because of the devil's consistent attacks. While operating in this mindset, without realizing it, I began to view these people and their prayers as the most important source of my spiritual strength. And I became a mediocre Christian, because I didn't fully accept the responsibility for my own spiritual growth. In seeking their prayers for the source of my strength, it left me open to the mercy of their vision and frailties.

Don't get me wrong, it's good to have Christian brothers and sisters to agree with you in prayer, but some religious people may not have your best interests at heart. So be very selective about who you have pray for your intimate needs. God has designed a system that allows you to build yourself up, whether someone else is available to pray with you or not.

When I asked for prayer in those early days, the power of God was dormant inside of me. In fact, the problems in my life got so bad I became suicidal. That's right, I was a suicidal child of God. What a terrible place to be. Finally, it became clear to me that relying on someone else to "pray my strength in the Lord" was making me spiritually weaker — not stronger. It simply didn't bring results.

Shortly after this crisis, someone showed me Jude 20. It was then that I found out I had the ability to "pray my own strength in the Lord." This verse says, "But ye, beloved, building up yourselves on your most holy faith, praying in the Holy Ghost." I found out that the best way to be strong in the Lord was for me to build myself up by praying in the Holy Spirit. And that no one, no matter how spiritual they are, can "pray your strength in the Lord." People can come against the enemy that is coming against you, but sooner or later you are going to have to build your own self up. That's why God put His power in you, not in someone else for you.

God's power may be in others around you, but He is in you to build you up. You can't, as I was led to believe, expect others to do it for you. As I began to build myself up by praying in the Holy Spirit daily as Jude 20 says, my circumstances began to change. They began to change because I finally began to tap into God's power that had been resident in me all along. And as I prayed in the Spirit, God's purpose, direction and calling became clearer and more exciting. Then, the Spirit of God in me began to dominate my flesh — the fears, emotions and selfish reasonings of my soul. As I began to yield to God's purpose, He began to reveal to me, through His Spirit, the steps that I needed to take toward the fulfillment of His vision for my life.

Learning about God's plan for my life alleviated all fear, and things began to work for good in the area of my finances, family and ministry.

As you begin to see yourself as a channel of blessing, you will begin to operate in God's power in you. God has given you this ability to help establish His covenant — to get His Word to people everywhere. So take His power to become a powerful manager in His Kingdom. This will fulfill God's call for your life and bring hope to many people.

For we dare not make ourselves of the number, or compare ourselves with some that commend themselves: but they measuring themselves by themselves, and comparing themselves among themselves, are not wise. But we will not boast of things without our measure, but according to the measure of the rule which God hath distributed to us, a measure to reach even unto you.
2 Corinthians 10:12,13

The calling of God upon you is unique. So it is critical that you pursue it. The lack of God's power in a believer's life can be attributed to a lack of vision. This is particularly true in ministry. It's easy to "spy" on other churches or ministries and compete with the vision God has given them. So don't allow that. And don't allow the enemy to take your focus off the vision that God has given you. As you seek God and pray for His direction, He will show you His unique vision for your life. He has already made provision for you to do what only *you* can do. And *the power in you* is more than enough to walk out to completion God's perfect will designed just for *you*. It will come to pass through His power in you. Make a new commitment today to seek and know Him intimately. Make a new commitment to share Him unashamedly. If you haven't known His power in you as He has always wanted you to, pray this very quick prayer now in faith with me.

"Father, I ask You now to forgive me of my sin and to fill me with Your power to be strong in You. I ask You to anoint me with Your Holy Spirit in a powerful way and to use me as a vessel of Your will. In Jesus' name."

Now, go and do mighty exploits in Jesus' name. Seek a church where God's Word is taught unashamedly and make a new commitment to study the Bible. Destroy the devil's works in your life, and make yourself available to help others get free. And pray every day in the language of God's Spirit to build yourself up in holy faith. The power in you is waiting for you to release His presence to change your life.

* * *

About the Author

Donald Shorter Sr. is pastor and founder of Pacific Christian Center, a vibrant, growing, non-denominational church in Tacoma, Washington. After leaving his successful secular radio and television broadcasting career, Don and his wife Kathy founded Pacific Christian Center in January of 1988.

Today Don and Kathy minister to thousands every week, through their regular weekly church services, radio and television broadcasts, and special teaching seminars. Donald Shorter, Sr. is best known for teaching the Word of God in a practical, powerful way, causing lifestyles to be miraculously changed. Together Don and Kathy Shorter are helping families to live *lifestyles of good success in every area of life*, through the Word of God. Write for a complete list of books, tapes and videos by Don and Kathy Shorter at this address:

Donald Shorter Ministries
Pacific Christian Center Worldwide Ministries
P. O. Box 44800
Tacoma, Washington 98444

Additional copies of this book are available from your local bookstore.

HARRISON HOUSE
Tulsa, Oklahoma 74153

In Canada books are available from:
Word Alive • P. O. Box 670
Niverville, Manitoba • CANADA R0A 1E0